YOUR PERSONALITY IN CHRIST

Understanding Your Position In Christ

Evangelist HARRISON JOHNSON UCHE

INTRODUCTION

Your personality is the real person inside you that people see whenever they see you as a child of God.

Personality can also be described as the greatness inside you, the real thing that lives in you that people will judge you by, and use to grade you whenever you say that you are a child of God.

Your personality is your value in life as a child of God.

CHAPTER ONE

John: 1 v 1-14: *In the beginning was the Word and the Word was with God, and the Word was God the same was in the beginning with God. All things were made by him; and without him was not anything made that was made. In him was life; and the life was the light of men. And the light shineth in darkness; and the darkness comprehended it not. There was a man sent from God, whose name was John. The same came for a witness, to bear witness of the Light that all men through him might believe. He was not that Light, but was sent to bear witness of that Light. That was the true Light, which lighteth every* *man that cometh into the world. He was in the world, and the world was made by him, and the world knew him not. He came unto his own, and his own received him not. But as many as received him, to them gave the power to become the sons of God, even to them that believe on his name: Which were born, not of blood, nor of the will of the flesh, nor of the will of man, but of God. And the Word was made flesh, and dwelt among us, (and we beheld his glory, the glory as of the only begotten of the Father) full of grace and truth.*

Any man that comes into this world has God's deposit which is the light of God (Christ) inside him. The Bible called it the light of God that shines upon any man that comes into this world. That means any soul that is born into this world either male or female has the mark of God upon him or her which is the deposit of God's plan upon every soul on earth.

Nobody is born empty into this world. God makes it a responsibility that you come into this world fully loaded with his blessing, to make sure that you are blessed and become a blessing to others which is God's plan for you.

But you can never discover what this deposit is until come back to God through his begotten son, Jesus Christ. Because God can never explain his deposit in your life to you until you become his son. He can then trust and reveal whatsoever deposit that he has deposited in you to you.

1Peter 2 v 2: *As newborn babes, desire the sincere milk of the word that ye may grow thereby:*

When you come to God through Christ and become saved, it does not end there, rather know that God expects you to grow in him and in a way you handle things, to reason and to have a change of mindset so as to grow in maturity of his divine nature in order to avoid been taken over by the lust of this world.

Meaning whenever you are saved, God expects you to work in the divine nature of his son, to be led by his Spirit.

Romans 8 v 12-14: *Therefore, brethren, we are debtors, not to the flesh, to live after the flesh. For if ye live after the flesh, ye shall die: but if ye through the Spirit do mortify the deeds of the* *body, ye shall live. For as many as are led by the Spirit of God, they are the sons of God.*

This is to avoid taking what is wrong as priority (The lust of the flesh) because whenever you say that you have received Christ as Lord and personal savior, there is supposed to be a change in everything you do. The way you talk, act and reason is supposed to be different from the way it used to be and that is what God wants to see in you whenever you are saved because God expects you to grow in behavior.

And for that growth to come or be seen in everything you do, you need to sit down and listen to the word of God.

Hebrews 4 v 12: *For the word of God is quick, and powerful, and sharper than any two edged sword, piercing even to the dividing asunder of soul and spirit, and of the joints and marrow, and is a discerner of the thoughts and intents of the heart.*

Because you can only understand yourself, God and discover your deposit in Christ when you have his word in you and you can never fail in anything you do in life.

Many people that fail to discover God's deposit upon their life are busy committing crimes because they are looking for a way to be satisfied which can never come until they agree to come back to God through Christ. As the scripture said that as many that received him even them that believe in his name has been given power to be called the children of God. Also the scripture said that Christ is full of grace and truth.

John 1 v 14-16: *And the Word was made flesh, and dwelt among us, (and we beheld his glory, the glory as of the only begotten of the Father,) full of grace and truth. John bare witness of him, and cried, saying, this was he of whom I spake, He that cometh after me is preferred before me: for he was before me. And of his fullness have all we received, and grace for grace.*

Whenever you believe in Christ, who is the word of God made flesh, and begin to eat it (study) you will grow in understanding to know your right from your left in Christ.

Grace is the deeper revelation of God's mystery in his word which Christ is full of: And through Christ you will understand the true mystery of what he really deposited in you, which is what made you whom you are.

Whenever you discover the deposit of God in your life, you will know your real value in life.

The sole reason why many people today are complaining, committing all sort of crimes, killing, stealing, drunkenness, prostitutions, gambling, and suicide is simply because they fail to discover what God's deposit in their life is and as such they don't know how valuable their life worth or whom they are before God or what God has created them to be here on earth.

1 John 4 v 17: *Herein is our love made perfect, that we may have boldness in the Day of Judgment: because as he is, so are we in this world.*

God created you in his image and left his mark, which is his deposit in you, but your failure to discover this value will lead you into holding wrong things and make what does not matter your priority and this will result in failure and complaints.

Discovering your deposit and knowing your value in life is what matters most and that is why God gave Jesus to you out of love to teach you how to discover yourself through his word.

Luke 4 v 18-19: *The Spirit of the Lord is upon me, because he hath anointed me to preach the gospel to the poor; he hath sent me to heal the brokenhearted, to preach deliverance to the captives, and recovering of sight to the blind, to set at liberty them that are bruised, To preach the acceptable year of the Lord.*

Jesus made this statement after he discovered himself and understood his ministry from the word of God, meaning for you to successfully discover yourself and know your value, it must be through the word of God. Your commitment to study the word of God makes him to reveal your deposit to you.

2 Peter 2 v 3: In their greed these teachers will exploit you with stories they have made up. Their condemnation has long been hanging over

them, and their destruction has not been sleeping.

2 Corinthians 3 v 18: *But we all, with open face beholding as in a glass the glory of the Lord, are changed into the same image from glory to glory, even as by the Spirit of the Lord.*

If you want to discover yourself and know your value or what God deposited in you, then you must be ready to study through the word of God. Then you will be able to know what God said about you and what he is saying about your situation at any point in time. God is not silent, he is still saying something in every situation but you can only hear and understand what he is saying through his word.

When you are studying the word of God, you are looking at yourself into God's mirror and that mirror is the glory of God. The word of God will mirror you into what it says about you; through it you will see your true identity, origin, heritage and deposit in Christ.

When the word of God mirrors you and shows you the deposit of God in you, your approach to things will change.

Maybe you might be thinking unworthy, living as if that you don't have a future or that you are not important on earth, but while studying the word of God, you will discover that you are so important and that you have a lot to offer and you will change and become a good person full of hope.

The word of God makes you to see things the way God see them. You will see people the way God sees them and not what they claim to be or where situations has placed them.

You will see from God's eyes and your judgment will be based on God's standard which will make you to always see the real deposit of God which is their personality and not the artificial created by the devil and his agents. Therefore, you will be able to understand every man, his value and worth before God and this discovering will cause you to love them the same way God love them.

Because discovering yourself gives you power to discover others and this discovering will always work for your glory.

Hebrews 4 v 13: *Neither is there any creature that is not manifest in his sight: but all things are naked and opened unto the eyes of him with whom we have to do.*

That is what the power of the word of God can do when you discover yourself through the word. The word of God is able to show you yourself and give you power to live accordingly. God's deeper revelation or mystery can only be revealed to you when Christ, which is the word of God, is living in you.

The truth is what God has deposited in you and this deposit in you is what Christ has come to reveal to you. That is why the devil is fighting to make sure that he takes you away from Christ (studying the word of God) because discovering who you are gives you power to live above all his traps and come out of his darkness.

Christ's mercy settles every issue and releases the grace to overcome sins. Christ came to restore a broken relationship between man and God, also to opens your eyes to discover your value, worth and personality. But without him, you will always see impossibility or hindrance in whatsoever thing you do.

Romans 8 v 19: *For the earnest expectation of the creature waiteth for the manifestation of the sons of God.*

The word of God will open your eyes to know whom you are, that you are no longer a condemned sinner rather that you have been made the righteousness of God through Christ, that you are the express image of God, that Jesus does not leave you at the mercy of the devil or circumstances of life to destroy you.

John 16 v 11: *Of judgment, because the prince of this world is judged.*

You will understand that the devil has been judged and sentenced and Christ has given you the power to deal with him, the way you like and you can cast him out at will.

Ephesians 2 v 6: *And hath raised us up together, and made us sit together in heavenly places in Christ Jesus:*

The word of God shows you that you are seated with the Lord Jesus in a place of power, far above every darkness, principalities and powers, occupying the place of authority in Christ far above Satan and everything that connects to him. This understanding and mystery will prompt you to know that you stand as God to this generation.

That you are no longer the same ordinary person that you used to be when you have not come to Christ and discover yourself; rather that God has made you hope of many hopeless men and women out there that are looking for upright men and women to depend on in times of problem.

You will discover your true identity that God has made you the hand to help the handless, the leg to the lame, and the eyes to so many blind people that want to see the glory of God.

Matthew 5 v 14: *Ye are the light of the world. A city that is set on a hill cannot be hid.*

This discovering will prompt you to see that so many people that are wandering in darkness today are waiting for nothing but for your light to you shine. You will understand that your light is the last hope of all the people that are covered with darkness and you will be forced to reach out and give them light.

You will discover that many people that are caged in demonic bondage through teachings and wrong doctrines that make the devil to sit on their heart, stopping them from understanding the truth about God and you will reach out to set them free through the word of God and the mystery you have understood.

James 5 v 16: *Confess your faults one to another, and pray one for another, that ye may be healed. The effectual fervent prayer of a righteous man availeth much.*

You will discover that a lot of sick people that are going from one hospital to the other hospital are waiting for your prayers to be healed because you will know that when you pray there will be instant healing. And you will be passionate to pray for them. You will make the case of others your prayer point and by doing so; God will always come to deliver you in your troubles.

Matthew 25 v 34 v 46: *Then shall the King say unto them on his right hand, Come, ye blessed of my Father, inherit the kingdom prepared for you from the foundation of the world: For I was an hungred, and ye gave me meat: I was thirsty,* and ye gave me drink: I was a stranger, and ye took me in: Naked, and ye clothed me: I was sick, and ye visited me: I was in prison, and ye came unto me. Then shall the righteous answer him, saying, Lord, when saw we thee hungred, and fed thee? Or thirsty, and gave thee drink? When saw we thee a stranger, and took thee in? Or naked, and clothed thee? Or when saw we thee sick, or in prison, and came unto thee? And the King shall answer and say unto them, Verily I say unto you, Inasmuch as ye have done it unto one of the least of these my brethren, ye have done it unto me. Then shall he say also unto them on the left hand, Depart from me, ye cursed, into everlasting fire, prepared for the devil and his angels: For I was an hungred, and ye gave me no meat: I was thirsty, and ye gave me no drink: I was a stranger, and ye took me not in: naked, and ye clothed me not: sick, and in prison, and ye visited me not. Then shall they also answer him, saying, Lord, when saw we thee a hungred, or athirst, or a stranger, or naked, or sick, or in prison, and did not minister unto thee? Then shall he answer them, saying, verily I say unto you, Inasmuch as ye did it not to one of the least of these, ye did it not to me. And these shall go away into *everlasting punishment: but the righteous into life eternal.*

You will discover that many people in the prison yards and orphanage homes needs your physical love and prayers everyday and you will be moved to visit and always pray for them. But whenever you don't know your value first, you can never see the need to add value to others.

Luke 4 v 18-19: *The Spirit of the Lord is upon me, because he hath anointed me to preach the gospel to the poor; he hath sent me to heal the brokenhearted, to preach deliverance to the captives, and recovering of sight to the blind, to set at liberty them that are bruised, To preach the acceptable year of the Lord.*

This is what Jesus said the day he discovered himself and understood the burden and need to add value to others.

Until you discover yourself, the deposit of God upon your life, you can never function well in your ministry, business, academics, career, marriage and finances.

It does not matter who you are, you might be in church and still be working in darkness, because without discovering your deposit you will lack direction in whatsoever thing you are doing. Even in the presence of a lifetime opportunity, you will be visionless and can never act in accordance to what God expects from you at any giving time.

John 8 v 12: *Then spake Jesus again unto them, saying, I am the light of the world: he that followeth me shall not walk in darkness, but shall have the light of life.*

Meaning that you can never make any impact in this world because you don't know yourself and don't have direction of what to do from God and this will prompt people to call you any name based on what they feel or think about you which is totally wrong from who God has made you.

Mark 8 v 27: *And Jesus went out, and his disciples, into the towns of Caesarea Philippi: and by the way he asked his disciples, saying unto them, who do men say that I am? And they answered, John the Baptist: but some say, Elias; and others, one of the prophets. And he saith unto them, But who say ye that I am? And Peter* *answereth and saith unto him, Thou art the Christ.*

Jesus asked his disciples this question to know what people think about him and when Peter said, "You are the son of God." Jesus told him that flesh and blood have not revealed this to you but you got this revelation by the Holy Spirit, meaning your real identity is that which God knows about you or who you are before God.

And your failure to discover this makes you see yourself as a failure. You will be incapacitated when things are going wrong in your life; marriage, church, nation, school and the devil will tell you that is normal and that there is nothing that you can do about it and you will be helpless in face of any problem.

Even as a child of God, you will see people dying every second without yet receiving Christ because nobody cared to preach the gospel to them and you will feel that is normal.

You will see the government making laws that are against the will of God and you will fold your hands watching and the devil will tell you that there is nothing wrong about it. When you are supposed to pray and stop it as the last hope of the world you are, the devil make you keep calm.

Matthew 5 v 14-16: *Ye are the light of the world. A city that is set on a hill cannot be hid. Neither do men light a candle, and put it under a bushel, but on a candlestick; and it giveth light unto all that are in the house. Let your light so shine before men, that they may see your good works, and glorify your Father which is in heaven.*

And as a light of the world, you are supposed to be the source which people around you will depend on to see in their darkness. But whenever you fail to discover yourself, you fail to understand that you can stop any negative situation around you through prayer.

James 5 v 17-18: *Elias was a man subject to like passions as we are, and he prayed earnestly that it might not rain: and it rained not on the earth by the space of three years and six months. And he prayed again, and the heaven gave rain, and the earth brought forth her fruit.*

So you can stop any bad government, change any wrong system in your nation, company, marriage, finance, academics, health, etc. through prayer, when you discover yourself in Christ and add the same value to others.

CHAPTER TWO

John 15 v 4-7: *Abide in me, and I in you. As the branch cannot bear fruit of itself, except it abide in the vine; no more can ye, except ye abide in me. I am the vine, ye are the branches: He that abideth in me, and I in him, the same bringeth forth much fruit: for without me ye can do nothing. If a man abides not in me, he is cast forth as a branch, and is withered; and men gather them, and cast them into the fire, and they are burned. If ye abide in me, and my words abide in you, ye shall ask what ye will, and it shall be done unto you.*

The difference between trees is its fruit and what attracts men to any tree is it's kind of fruit. That means every tree has its kind of fruit either bad or good fruit and this fruit is what will determine the kind of people or animals that will be attracted to the tree.

Jesus said. "If you are in me, you will bring much fruits," meaning every human being on earth must have a fruit that people will see and be attracted to them.

And your fruit depends on the type of tree that you are. A mango tree can never bring banana fruit. Jesus said, "I am the true vine and people that have my revelation and mystery in them are my branches and they will bring much fruits," meaning not one type of fruit rather they will have many types of fruit that will attract different kind of people to them and these people will come with whatsoever they have and hand it over to them.

Matthew 6 v 33: *But seek ye first the kingdom of God, and his righteousness; and all these things shall be added unto you.*

Seek first to remain in me and you will bring fruit that will attract men with whatsoever you need in life to you, because when you learn from Christ, you will be announced into glory. When Christ teaches you through his word, your glory will show forth.

Proverbs 18 v 16: *A man's gift maketh room for him, and bringeth him before great men.*

You don't struggle to be noticed by men whenever you discover yourself, all you need is to remain in Christ and your fruit will attract men to you. Everybody wants to identify with success and wherever people see anything that looks like that success in you, they will be running after you and that is why the devil is faking success to make it look as if there is success outside Christ.

But when you sit down to check very well, you will discover that a lot of people that are parading as superstars, millionaires, and inventors, which many people are using as role models, are passing through depression, addictions of different types and at times you see many of them committing suicide, seeking for divorce in search of peace. Why? Because the devil can never give a better fruit that will remain and his fake success does not grant lasting peace.

John 14 v 27: *Peace I leave with you, my peace I give unto you: not as the world giveth, give I unto you. Let not your heart be troubled, neither let it be afraid.*

Many people are disappointed today because the candidate they believed so much on and voted for in the last election thinking that he/she will bring peace and solutions to their lives has failed to do so.

So many people can speak peacefully to you from afar but whenever you go close to them or bring them close to your family, you will begin to see different things.

You may think that many people are successful but when you go close to them, you discover that they are in a big mess and are crying day and night. Why? because devil has neither success nor peace in him. The Bible calls him wolves in sheep clothing.

Psalm 73 v 2-28: *But as for me, my feet were almost gone; my steps had well nighslipped. For I* *was envious at the foolish, when I saw the prosperity of the wicked. For there are no bands in their death: but their strength is firm. They are not in trouble as other men; neither are they plagued like other men. Therefore pride compasseth them about as a chain; violence covereth them as a garment. Their eyes stand out with fatness: they have more than heart could wish. They are corrupt, and speak wickedly concerning oppression: they speak loftily. They set their mouth against the heavens, and their tongue walketh through the earth. Therefore his people return hither: and waters of a full cup are wrung out to them. And they say, how doth God know? And is there knowledge in the most High? Behold, these are the ungodly, who prosper in the world; they increase in riches. Verily I have cleansed my heart in vain, and washed my hands in innocency. For all the day long have I been plagued, and chastened every morning. If I say, I will speak thus; behold, I should offend against the generation of thy children. When I thought to know this, it was too painful for me; until I went into the sanctuary of God; then understood I their end. Surely thou didst set them in slippery places: thou castedst them down into destruction. How are they brought into desolation, as in a moment! They are utterly consumed with terrors. As a dream when one awaketh; so, O Lord, when thou awakest, thou shalt despise their image. Thus my heart was grieved, and I was pricked in my reins. So foolish was I, and ignorant: I was as a beast before thee. Nevertheless I am continually with thee: thou hast holden me by my right hand. Thou shalt guide me with thy counsel, and afterward receive me to glory. Whom have I in heaven but thee? And there is none upon earth that I desire beside thee. My flesh and my heart faileth: but God is the strength of my heart, and my portion forever. For, lo, they that are far from thee shall perish: thou hast destroyed all them that go a whoring from thee. But it is good for me to draw near to God: I have put my trust in the Lord GOD, that I may declare all thy works.*

But when you remain rooted in Christ and discover yourself, you will not be moved by the fake success of the heathen which has taken many people away from God and even caused them to question the love of God over their life. You will not be moved by sight but rather by what God says about you because you know that whatsoever he says must come to pass in your life.

Zephaniah 3 v 17-20: *The LORD thy God in the midst of thee is mighty; he will save, he will rejoice over thee with joy; he will rest in his love, he will joy over thee with singing. I will gather them that are sorrowful for the solemn assembly, who are of thee, to whom the reproach of it was a burden. Behold, at that time I will undo all that afflict thee: and I will save her that halteth, and gather her that was driven out; and I will get them praise and fame in every land where they have been put to shame. At that time will I bring you again, even in the time that I gather you: for I will make you a name and praise among all people of the earth, when I turn back your captivity before your eyes, saith the LORD.*

But if you continue to remain with the Lord, you will come to know that God is excited about you. All that is required from you is to trust his righteousness. Accepting and receiving his righteousness into your spirit makes you to be blessed in him and transformed into what he says you are.

Romans 6 v 14: *For sin shall not have dominion over you: for ye are not under the law, but under grace.*

Accepting his righteousness into your spirit breaks the power of sin over your life, thereby given way for his spirit to engulf and dwell in you at all times.

Whenever his spirit dwells in you, you will gradually change into what he has made you to be and you will have the full nature of Christ thereby causing his Holy Spirit to be fully at work in you and he will work to make sure that you are successful in everything you do in this life.

His presence in your life makes it easy for you to enjoy a rich fellowship with the Father and bring much fruit in all your labor on earth.

Because you will be receiving direct information from heaven, thus you will always be connected to the throne of God which is the throne of success, wisdom, understanding, knowledge, power, peace, joy and love.

John 5 v 19-23: *Then answered Jesus and said unto them, "Verily, verily, I say unto you, the*

Son can do nothing of himself, but what he seeth the Father do: for what things so ever he doeth, these also doeth the Son likewise. For the Father loveth the Son, and showeth him all things that himself doeth: and he will shew him greater works than these that ye may marvel. For as the Father raiseth up the dead, and quickeneth them; even so the Son quickeneth whom he will. For the Father judgeth no man, but hath committed all judgment unto the Son: That all men should honor the Son, even as they honor the Father. He that honoureth not the Son honoureth not the Father which hath sent him."

Your relationship with the father will be that of Christ and his father. You will not be far from the truth of what God is saying in every situation at all time that means, you will have rightful knowledge on what to do at any point in time. Nobody will outshine you or intimidate you in anyway because you are connected to the throne of God.

John 14 v 16-18: *And I will pray the Father, and he shall give you another Comforter, that he may abide with you forever; Even the Spirit of truth; whom the world cannot receive, because it* *seeth him not, neither knoweth him: but ye know him; for hedwelleth with you, and shall be in you. I will not leave you comfortless: I will come to you.*

The Holy Spirit will be there to teach you how to understand and obey the voice of God and enjoy an intimate relationship with the Father to achieve success that comes from his abiding presence when you enjoy a good relationship with him.

Galatians 5 v 22-23: *But the fruit of the Spirit is love, joy, peace, longsuffering, gentleness, goodness, faith, Meekness, temperance: against such there is no law.*

That means as you remain connected to Christ through his Holy Spirit which is the indwelling presence the father in your life, he will bring out the fruits in you.

That is why Jesus said that if you remain in me and I in you, you will bring out much fruits. And these fruits (success, wisdom, understanding, knowledge, power, peace, joy and love) are what many people will see and know that you are a child of God and be attracted to you.

Your fruit is what attracts people to you, your fruit is what people will see and judge you by and when they judge from your fruit they judge correctly.

Matthew 7 v 16: *Ye shall know them by their fruits. Do men gather grapes of thorns, or figs of thistles?*

People will judge you from whatsoever fruit you bear, that is why Jesus said if you want to serve me, it must be in truth and in spirit.

If the Holy Spirit is already in you, the truth is the fruit that the Holy Spirit will bring out in you that people will see in you and know who you are.

The truth is those fruits mentioned in the above scripture which when is in you, people will see it and know that you have them, you cannot fake them either.

As a man cannot say that he feels like a man, because a man knows that he is a man and will always think like a man any day, any time, to be a man is not a feeling and he can't feel it rather he is sure that he is a man. That is how it is when you have the spirit of God and allow him to dwell in you; all his fruits mentioned in the above scripture will be seen in you.

You don't feel it; you can't say I feel love. "No," love is not a feeling, love is your nature, is part of your DNA in Christ. When you are in Christ and discover yourself, you can't feel peace and joy; rather you have them in you. It is not a feeling, it is part of your nature which you are sure to have even at night.

You cannot go about telling people with your mouth that you love them because when they see you they will see love, as people will always see the difference between a man and woman, so they can see a difference in you from other people, because when they see you they will see love.

Remember that Jesus said by their fruit not by their confession because when people see you, they will see joy and peace in you not when you claim it.

Though they may not come and tell you instantly, but from afar they will always testify that you are a man of peace, etc. and when they are in trouble and need peace, they will be attracted to you because of your peace.

Millions of people that are looking for a peaceful environment to operate will come and identify with you whenever they notice you. People will see your gentleness, how easily you are to deal with, your meekness which is your humanity; down to earth, thus no matter how much you have in life you are still humble.

Your longsuffering in the face of provocation, your faith in God when it seems that all hope is lost in life, and they will be amazed and be attracted to you.

They are coming to you because they are convinced that you can add value to their life and they will be ready to pay any amount to receive that value in their life.

And they are not coming to you empty handed, rather they are coming to surrender all they have to you in other to receive your value.

Isaiah 49 v 23: *And kings shall be thy nursing fathers, and their queens thy nursing mothers: they shall bow down to thee with their face toward the earth, and lick up the dust of thy feet; and thou shalt know that I am the LORD: for they shall not be ashamed that wait for me.*

Thus a lawyer will come to you and submit his wisdom. Company owners will come to you, rich men and women of all capacity, kings, queens, doctors and directors of different things will come, seeking to submit all they have to you because they saw your fruits and became attracted to it.

Colossians 2 v 10: *And ye are complete in him, which is the head of all principality and power.*

Ephesians 1 v 21: *Far above all principality, and power, and might, and dominion, and every name that is named, not only in this world, but also in that which is to come.*

Satan and all his agents will be under your feet because your kind of fruit is poison to them.

Psalm 1 v 4: *Blessed is the man that walketh not in the counsel of the ungodly, nor standeth in* *the way of sinners, nor sitteth in the seat of the scornful. But his delight is in the law of the LORD; and in his law doth he meditate day and night. And he shall be like a tree planted by the rivers of water, that bringeth forth his fruit in his season; his leaf also shall not wither; and whatsoever he doeth shall prosper.*

When you continue remaining in Christ, you increase in fruit and attract money and more people into the kingdom of God and build a big financial empire that people will be surprised on how it comes to be.

Many reputable men and women will be willing to invest in you and serve your interest and make sure that you succeed and fulfill your God given mandate on earth.

This is why Jesus said that you should seek to fit in the kingdom of God first because whenever you come to this level you will discover yourself and every other thing that you require will be yours.

1 Corinthians 3 v 21: *Therefore, let no man glory in men. For all things are yours.*

Jesus knows that whatsoever thing that you are looking for on earth, men and women will bring it to you free of charge when you remain in him and build your spiritual life and have total nature of Christ in you.

Romans 8 v 17: *And if children, then heirs; heirs of God, and joint-heirs with Christ; if so be that we suffer with him, that we may be also glorified together.*

Any type of riches, money, cars and things you can mention, as long as they are here on earth, will be attracted to you through your fruit of your spirit. Because all blessings are yours and freely given to you in Christ (1 Corinthians 3 v 21) but to receive it you must be acquainted with the Holy Spirit so that his fruit will come out in you and when people see the fruit they will not have any other option than to follow you.

Mark 16 v 17-18: *And these signs shall follow them that believe; in my name shall they cast out devils; they shall speak with new tongues; they shall take up serpents; and if they drink any deadly thing, it shall not hurt them;*

they shall lay hands on the sick, and they shall recover.

Even when they seem not to love you, they cannot resist you because they cannot do without you because of your fruit, so they will not have another option other than to follow you against their wishes because you are their last hope.

During his earthly ministering, Jesus makes this remark and told the crowd following him that they are following him because of the great miracles that he was doing and not because they love him.

That means your fruit will force many people to follow you and surrender their wealth to you because they want to receive from your fruit and when you give them, they gather their own and give back to you in return.

Luke 6 v 38: *Give, and it shall be given unto you; good measure, pressed down, and shaken together, and running over, shall men give into your bosom. For with the same measure that ye mete withal it shall be measured to you again.*

Hebrews 7 v 7: *And without all contradiction the less is blessed of the better.*

When you give them your gift, Jesus said the same way they shall give back to you. Remember, he didn't say one person but he said shall men give back to you, as millions of people who buy this book has given to my life, the Bible said shaking together shall they give to my bosom because I have given to them first. That is the reason the Holy Spirit makes you to be fruitful.

Your fruit is your source of income from God which you use to promote the kingdom of God in return.

Deuteronomy 28 v 4: *Blessed shall be the fruit of thy body, and the fruit of thy ground, and the fruit of thy cattle, the increase of thy kind, and the flocks of thy sheep.*

So seek to remain in him and be filled with his spirit to bring out good fruits that will attract people to the kingdom of God.

CHAPTER THREE

Your inability to remain connected to Christ makes Christ to cut you off from the tree of life and you will become prey to the devil and his agents who will mesmerize you the way they like.

Even as a Christian, when you are not connected to Christ through his Spirit to learn from him, the devil will use his agents who are also working to promote his kingdom to deceive you and make you suffer loss here on earth and in hell hereafter.

2 Peter 2 v 1-4: *But there were false prophets also among the people, even as there shall be false teachers among you, who privily shall bring in damnable heresies, even denying the Lord that bought them, and bring upon themselves swift destruction. And many shall follow their pernicious ways; by reason of which the way of truth shall be evil spoken of. And through covetousness shall they with feigned words make merchandise of you: whose judgment now of a long time lingereth not, and their damnation slumbereth not. For if God spared not the angels that sinned, but cast them down to hell, and delivered them into chains of darkness, to be reserved unto judgment.*

These are ministers of the devil that are parading themselves as the ministers of God in order to deceive many that are disconnected from the tree of life which is Christ.

Matthew 23 v 13: *But woe unto you, scribes and Pharisees, hypocrites! For ye shut up the kingdom of heaven against men: for ye neither go in yourselves, neither suffer ye them that are entering to go in.*

Many people who are saying that life is boring today, that are complaining how things are in their marriage, finances, family, business, career, etc. Are doing so because they are disconnected from Christ and at such they could not discover their deposit from God.

1 Peter 2 v 2: *As newborn babes, desire the sincere milk of the word that ye may grow thereby.*

This type of Christians could not grow because they fail to eat food of the spirit; they lack nutrition as they are disconnected from Christ through his word. These types of Christians are in the church but they cannot grow in spirit.

And they will be the same way as they were when they came new to the church. They are there complaining and looking for a miracle that will change their lives without looking to discover their deposit in Christ by connecting to him through his word.

John 1 v 9-12: *That was the true Light, which lighteth every man that cometh into the world. He was in the world, and the world was* *made by him, and the world knew him not. He came unto his own, and his own received him not. But as many as received him, to them gave the power to become the sons of God, even to them that believe on his name.*

And their problem is not because they have not received Christ !they are born again because they have confessed Jesus Christ as their Lord and personal Savior and they believed in his name and are born into the kingdom of God. But as a baby, they need to eat the food of the spirit which is the word of God to grow grown and become a son in the family of God; to know their right from their left but because they are not eating the word thereby remain as babies every day even in the church.

Galatians 4 v 1-3: *Now I say, that the heir, as long as he is a child, differeth nothing from a servant, though he be lord of all; but is under tutors and governors until the time appointed of the father. Even so we, when we were children, were in bondage under the elements of the world.*

Giving your life to Christ in the first place prompts God to take over your soul from the devil but for God's spirit to merge with your spirit and dwell in your flesh; do his work through you must be by your choice to work it out by eating the word of God.

Philippians 2 v 12: *Wherefore, my beloved, as ye have always obeyed, not as in my presence only, but now much more in my absence, work out your own salvation with fear and trembling.*

Whenever you don't desire the food of the spirit, there is no way God can force you to do so, rather you will be left at the mercy of the devil that will capture you through his agents and they will keep you bound for some many years without result. They will cause you limitation in your career, marriage, finances, academics, business, health, ministry, etc. Because as a baby, these agents of the devil can teach you anything they like and still make you pay heavily in cash because their aim is to make money from you, destroy your future and make sure that you don't discover yourself and God's deposit in your life.

They know that whenever you grow to a level where you can discover yourself and your deposit then you will know your personality and who you are in Christ and then you will be set free from their cage, torment and bondage.

That is why they are not teaching you a sound word of God rather they are preaching miracles and prosperity to you knowing full well that without having the word of God in you, that miracle and prosperity will not last.

Romans 8 v 14: *For as many as are led by the Spirit of God, they are the sons of God.*

They are doing this to stop you from growing from a child of God to a son of God because they know that the spirit of God only led the sons of God also that God can only reveal his mysteries, cause signs and wonders to follow to his sons. That means there are no way you can discover yourself and know your deposit when you are following them

And If you cannot discover your value, you cannot add value to your life or to others in your family, so you will depend on them and they will keep deceiving you and making merchandise of you, manipulating your blessing through their demonic and diabolic means.

Without knowing your value, you cannot add value to other people's life, and not knowing your value gives other people the opportunity to discover your value and make money becoming influential because of your ignorance. Thus your inability to study and stay connected to Christ to discover your deposit makes others (fake pastors and prophets) to discover you as a good costumer to enrich them-selves, be influential and leave a legacy for their unborn generation.

Mark 16 v 17- 18: *And these signs shall follow them that believe; in my name shall they cast out devils; they shall speak with new tongues; they shall take up serpents; and if they drink any deadly thing, it shall not hurt them; they shall lay hands on the sick, and they shall recover.*

But because you don't know your value and have not discovered your deposit, that is why you are running after miracles that are supposed to follow you everywhere you go when you discover yourself and know your value in Christ.

Isaiah 30: *Woe to the rebellious children, saith the LORD, that take counsel, but not of me; and that cover with a covering, but not of my spirit, that they may add sin to sin: That walk to go down into Egypt, and have not asked at my mouth; to strengthen themselves in the strength of Pharaoh, and to trust in the shadow of Egypt! Therefore shall the strength of Pharaoh be your shame, and the trust in the shadow of Egypt your confusion. For his princes were at Zoan, and his ambassadors came to Hanes. They were all ashamed of a people that could not profit them, nor be a help nor profit, but a shame, and also a reproach. The burden of the beasts of the south: into the land of trouble and anguish, from whence come the young and old lion, the viper and fiery flying serpent, they will carry their riches upon the shoulders of young asses, and their treasures upon the bunches of camels, to a people that shall not profit them. For the Egyptians shall help in vain, and to no purpose: therefore have I cried concerning this, their strength is to sit still. Now go, write it before them in a table, and note it in a book that it may be for the time to come for ever and ever: That this is a rebellious people, lying children, children* *that will not hear the law of the LORD: Which say to the seers, See not; and to the prophets, prophesy not unto us right things, speak unto us smooth things, prophesy deceits: Get you out of the way, turn aside out of the path, and cause the Holy One of Israel to cease from before us. Wherefore thus saith the Holy One of Israel, because ye despise this word, and trust in oppression and perverseness, and stay thereon: Therefore this iniquity shall be to you as a breach ready to fall, swelling out in a high wall, whose breaking cometh suddenly at an instant. And he shall break it as the breaking of the potters' vessel that is broken in pieces; he shall not spare: so that there shall not be found in the bursting of it a sherd to take fire from the hearth, or to take water withal out of the pit. For thus saith the Lord GOD, the Holy One of Israel; in returning and rest shall ye be saved; in quietness and in confidence shall be your strength: and ye would not. But ye said, No; for we will flee upon horses; therefore shall ye flee: and, we will ride upon the swift; therefore shall they that pursue you be swift. One thousand shall flee at the rebuke of one; at the rebuke of five shall ye flee: till ye be left as a beacon upon the top of a mountain, and as an ensign on a hill. And therefore will the LORD wait, that he may be gracious unto you, and therefore will he be exalted, that he may have mercy upon you: for the LORD is a God of judgment: blessed are all they that wait for him. For the people shall dwell in Zion at Jerusalem: thou shalt weep no more: he will be very gracious unto thee at the voice of thy cry; when he shall hear it, he will answer thee. And though the Lord give you the bread of adversity, and the water of affliction, yet shall not thy teachers be removed into a corner anymore, but thine eyes shall see thy teachers: And thine ears shall hear a word behind thee, saying, this is the way, walk ye in it, when ye turn to the right hand, and when ye turn to the left. Ye shall defile also the covering of thy graven images of silver, and the ornament of thy molten images of gold: thou shalt cast them away as a menstruous cloth; thou shalt say unto it, get thee hence. Then shall he give the rain of thy seed that thou shalt sow the ground withal; and bread of the increase of the earth, and it shall be fat and plenteous: in that day shall thy cattle feed in large pastures. The oxen likewise and the young asses that ear the ground shall eat clean provender, which hath been winnowed with the shovel and with the fan. And there shall be upon every high mountain and upon every high hill, rivers and streams of waters in the day of the great slaughter, when the towers fall. Moreover the light of the moon shall be as the light of the sun, and the light of the sun shall be sevenfold, as the light of seven days, in the day that the LORD bindeth up the breach of his people, and healeth the stroke of their wound. Behold, the name of the LORD cometh from far, burning with his anger, and the burden thereof is heavy: his lips are full of indignation, and his tongue as a devouring fire: And his breath, as an overflowing stream, shall reach to the midst of the neck, to sift the nations with the sieve of vanity: and there shall be a bridle in the jaws of the people, causing them to err. Ye shall have a song, as in the night when a holy solemnity is kept; and gladness of heart, as when one goeth with a pipe to come into the mountain of the LORD, to the mighty One of Israel. And the LORD shall cause his glorious voice to be heard, and shall shew the lighting down of his arm, with the indignation of his anger, and with the flame of a devouring fire, with scattering, and tempest, and hailstones. For through the voice of the LORD shall the Assyrian be beaten down, which smote with a rod. And in every place where the grounded staff shall pass, which the LORD shall lay upon him, it shall be with tablets and harps: and in battles of shaking will he fight with it. For Tophet is ordained of old; yea, for the king it is prepared; he hath made it deep and large: the pile thereof is fire and much wood; the breath of the LORD, like a stream of brimstone, doth kindle it.*

And running after this miracle takes you away to the wrong alter where they will deceive you in the name of the Lord. Because many people are running after miracles, they always end up adding more problems to themselves without knowing it. They will cover you with another spirit that is not the spirit of God, which will create more problem than solving the old one.

Many marriages have been broken today because in the process of running after miracles they step to an unholy alter. Many families are suffering today because they are running after miracles, many business and relationships has collapsed because of running after miracle. Instead of sitting down to study the word of

God to grow and discover their value in Christ, people are running after miracles, without knowing that there is no short cut to success rather this is the trap of the devil to distract them from been connected to Christ, which is the source of what they want in life.

Signs and wonders shall follow them, meaning it will follow everybody that is willing to study and obey him and it is not limited to pastors or big men of God only. Studying the word of God gives you direct access to know any information from God. Remember the word is the same today and forever but miracles can fail, that means if you stay connected to Christ you will have any information that will produce the miracle you are looking for in life.

In fact, any miracle you receive today from any man of God, no matter how anointed the person is, must be maintained by the word of God or else you will lose that miracle later.

Remember, your inability to discover your value in Christ creates opportunity for others to discover you value and use it to make money. You are looking for miracles while the fake pastors see you as a good costumer and you will pay for your ignorance.

Hosea 4 v 6: *My people are destroyed for lack of knowledge: because thou hast rejected knowledge, I will also reject thee, that thou shalt be no priest to me: seeing thou hast forgotten the law of thy God, I will also forget thy children.*

That means the devil is not mesmerizing because he has power but because of your ignorance on what to do to discover yourself and remain connected to Christ and grow as a good tree, fill with his spirit to bring forth fruits that will attract the entire miracle that you are looking for.

Galatians 5 v 22-23: *But the fruit of the Spirit is love, joy, peace, longsuffering, gentleness, goodness, faith, Meekness, temperance: against such there is no law.*

Remember, miracles are supposed to be following you, not you following after miracles. So when are connected to God, you will be filled with his spirit and all the fruits of the spirit will be seen in you and these fruits will attract your miracle. But lack of knowledge about this mystery creates opportunity for the devil and his agents to take over you and make life miserable for you here on earth.

3 John 1 v 2: *Beloved, I wish above all things that thou mayest prosper and be in health, even as thy soul prospereth.*

God might be looking for a way to reach out and help you but without sitting down and studying to know the area or what his instructions are at any moment, there is no way such blessing will reach you. Because the only medium that God will use to pass his information to you must be through his word that is why if you don't sit down to hear his voice you cannot know what he is saying.

Romans 8 v 15-17: *For ye have not received the spirit of bondage again to fear; but ye have received the Spirit of adoption, whereby we cry, Abba, Father. The Spirit itself beareth witness with our spirit, that we are the children of God: And if children, then heirs; heirs of God, and joint-heirs with Christ; if so be that we suffer with him, that we may be also glorified together.*

Understand that from the moment you gave your life to Christ that God has blessed you and made you joint heir with Christ.

1 Corinthians 2 v 12-14: *Now we have received, not the spirit of the world, but the spirit which is of God; that we might know the things that are freely given to us of God. Which things also we speak, not in the words which man's wisdom teacheth, but which the Holy Ghost teacheth; comparing spiritual things with spiritual. But the natural man receiveth not the things of the Spirit of God: for they are foolishness unto him: neither can he know them, because they are spiritually discerned.*

But there is no way you can enjoy the wealth given to you until you know yourself, the Holy Spirit and stay in fellowship with the Father and with the son, Jesus Christ, which is the word.

1 Corinthians 3 v 21: *Therefore let no man glory in men. For all things are yours.*

When you grow and know your deposit, the Holy Spirit will reveal all God's blessing to you. All you need is to take advantage of his ministry in your life, stay connected to the Father and develop a strong personal relationship with him.

Until you get to know him, you can never be liberated from the torment of the devil and his agents. And the devil knows that the only way you can come out of darkness and live above his trap is getting this revelation from the word of God.

That is why he is trying all he can to stop you or distract you from sitting down and hearing from God. Because God's word is the only tool that have exposed his kingdom. Jesus made open show of the devil and triumphed over him and whenever you have this deeper knowledge and revelation through his word, you will be above the devil and his torments.

John 1 v 9: *That was the true light, which lighteth every man that cometh into the world.*

Meaning the only thing that can destroy the power of darkness in your life completely is not fasting and praying only but your deeper revelation of God through his word which is filled with his spirit.

So when you get connected to God through Christ (who is the word of God made flesh) and his Holy Spirit will teach you to understand his deeper revelation and you will discover your deposit from him which will make you to be free and live above every demonic attack here on earth.

John 16 v 11: *Of judgment, because the prince of this world is judged.*

The devil has been defeated, so stop disturbing yourself about him. He is not your problem; all you need is to get the rightful knowledge of who you are and whom God has made you, then you will put the devil where he belongs which is under your feet.

CHAPTER FOUR

Luke 4 v 18-29: *The Spirit of the Lord is upon me, because he hath anointed me to preach the gospel to the poor; he hath sent me to heal the brokenhearted, to preach deliverance to the captives, and recovering of sight to the blind, to set at liberty them that are bruised, To preach the acceptable year of the Lord. And he closed the book, and he gave it again to the minister, and sat down. And the eyes of all them that were in the synagogue were fastened on him. And he began to say unto them, this day is this scripture fulfilled in your ears. And all bare him witness, and wondered at the gracious words which* *proceeded out of his mouth. And they said, is not this Joseph's son? And he said unto them, ye will surely say unto me this proverb, 'Physician, heal thyself: whatsoever we have heard done in Capernaum, do also here in thy country.' And he said, 'Verily I say unto you, No prophet is accepted in his own country. But I tell you of a truth, many widows were in Israel in the days of Elias; when the heaven was shut up three years and six months, when great famine was throughout all the land; but unto none of them was Elias sent, save unto Sarepta, a city of Sidon, unto a woman that was a widow. And many lepers were in Israel in the time of Eliseus the prophet; and none of them was cleansed, saving Naaman the Syrian. And all they in the synagogue, when they heard these things, were filled with wrath, And rose up, and thrust him out of the city, and led him unto the brow of the hill whereon their city was built, that they might cast him down headlong. But he passing through the midst of them went his way.'*

Our Lord Jesus was able to discover himself through the word of God. The Bible said he came to the synagogue as his custom was! That means he has been studying through the word of God seeking to discover himself through the word and after discovering himself the Bible recorded that he grew in knowledge and in power.

Seeking to discover yourself through the word of God keeps you in touch and connected to God through his word. Whenever you are committed to study and wait unto God through his word, you will grow in statue in every area of your life.

Meaning for you to experience growth in your business, marriage, finances, job, career, etc. know that it must be by studying the word of God to discover yourself and know what to do at any given time.

Because whatsoever it takes for you to be the best which the Lord has made you is not anywhere rather it is deposited inside of you and until you discover it, the growth and the blessing that you are looking for will not come.

John 1 v 9: *That was the true Light, which lighteth every man that cometh into the world.*

The whole miracle that you are looking for is deposited in you even before you came into this world, but for you to discover it and live in fullness of it must be through the word of God,it is in the place of study to discover yourself that you will receive the anointing that will explain who you are, where you are going and how to go about it to you.

1 John 2 v 27: *But the anointing which ye have received of him abideth in you, and ye need not that any man teach you: but as the same anointing teacheth you of all things, and is truth, and is no lie, and even as it hath taught you, ye shall abide in him.*

This anointing will teach you how to come out of whatsoever problem you will be faced with as a child of God and whatsoever the anointing teaches is nothing but the truth, so whenever you listen and obey him, he will lead you from nowhere to your glory.

Until you discover yourself in God and ready to obey him, you can never know what God wants from you. You will be living here on earth with direction, confused without knowing what to do and what God wants from you or how he wants you to relate to people and how to receive your benefits from him as his child.

When Jesus discovers himself from the word of God, he got the revelation of what God wanted from him. He understood exactly why he was here on earth and that was to set the captives free, preach the Good News to the poor, and heal the sick, etc.

Whenever you discover your deposit, the picture of your assignment on earth will be given to you by God. Jesus was able to fulfill his assignment here on earth because he was able to discover himself and know what his assignment was all about.

Discovering yourself will make you to know the importance of others, because soon as you discover yourself, you will discover the value of others. People you thought were of less importance to you will matter much to you because you will discover that they are very important to your life. Example: when you discover that God has made you a pastor, you will discover that the sinners that you are thinking to be less important will matter much to you because you need make them repent to become your members and as well help you in your ministry to build the Kingdom of God.

When you discover that you are a leader, you will discover that you need them to be your followers because you cannot be a good leader without followers.

If you discover that you are a mechanic, you will discover that you need car owners to be your costumers thereby you pray and help others to buy car if possible. If you discover that you are a business owner, you will discover that you need others as your costumers. You will see the reason why God has made you and placed you in any position and why he has allowed some situations to happen around you.

And you will see why you should value others and respect them because they are important to your life too.

Matthew 22 v 39: *And the second is like unto it, Thou shalt love thy neighbor as thyself.*

The Bible says that because God knows that if you can discover yourself, you will discover the role and importance of your neighbors in your life and you will see reasons to love them as yourself because your life is meaningless without others.

But it will be impossible for you to love your neighbors when you have not discovered their value to your life and for you to discover their value, you have to discover yourself value first and this must be by constant studying of the word of God.

The word of God is the only thing that will guide you to discover yourself and the value of others in your life.

And until you discover their value you can never benefit from them.

Romans 12 v 18-21: *If it be possible, as much as lieth in you, live peaceably with all men. Dearly beloved, avenge not yourselves, but rather give place unto wrath: for it is written, vengeance is mine; I will repay, saith the Lord. Therefore if thine enemy hunger, feed him; if he thirst, give him drink: for in so doing thou shalt heap coals of fire on his head. Be not overcome of evil, but overcome evil with good.*

Whenever you discover your role in the life of others and how useful they can be to you, you will come to the understanding to know that there is no need to be at war with anybody. The most successful people on earth are people who discovered the value of others and made use of them to become successful.

From age's, successful men and women have used other people as a tool or ladder to climb to a higher level in order to be successful, **wealthy**, and influential, and to leave a legacy for their unborn generation.

2 Peter 2 v 2-3: *And many shall follow their pernicious ways; by reason of which the way of truth shall be evil spoken of. And through covetousness shall they with feigned words make merchandise of you: whose judgment now of a long time lingereth not, and their damnation slumbereth not.*

A foolish man is prisoner of a wise man's thought, so your inability to discover God's position in your life leaves you at the mercy of others to discover you and they will become your task masters.

CHAPTER FIVE

Geneses 37 v 5-11: *And Joseph dreamed a dream, and he told it his brethren: and they hated him yet the more. And he said unto them, 'Hear, I pray you, this dream which I have dreamed: For, behold, we were binding sheaves in the field, and, lo, my sheaf arose, and also stood upright; and, behold, your sheaves stood round about, and made obeisance to my sheaf.' And his brethren said to him, 'Shalt thou indeed reign over us? Or shalt thou indeed have dominion over us?' And they hated him yet the more for his dreams, and for his words. And he dreamed yet another dream, and told it his brethren, and said,*

'Behold, I have dreamed a dream more; and, behold, the sun and the moon and the eleven stars made obeisance to me.' And he told it to his father, and to his brethren: and his father rebuked him, and said unto him, 'What is this dream that thou hast dreamed? Shall I and thy mother and thy brethren indeed come to bow down ourselves to thee to the earth?' And his brethren envied him; but his father observed the saying.

The story of Joseph and his brethren is a popular story in the Bible that everybody knows; it is also a historic story of the Jew's nation. What I want to point out there is the attitude of Joseph's brothers. They hated him because of his dream.

Joseph had a dream of becoming a king and told his brothers with a very open heart, thinking that the dream would go over well with them. But instead of causing happiness, the dream became a stepping stone for them to destroy them.

People that he thought would help him to make his dream become a reality turned out to hate him and were seeking for a way to make sure that his dream never sees the light of the day.

Their sole aim was to make sure that Joseph will be frustrated and his dream to be destroyed. And they were not doing it to receive anything as a benefit for their work or to short cut Joseph and step into his shoes to become the King instead but they were doing it to make sure that Joseph will not be greater than them or rule over them.

The role played by Joseph's brothers is a clear example of men that has never discovered them-selves. Men that doesn't know their value in life.

Today, many people are like this Joseph's brothers, they are parading themselves in our churches, schools, offices, community and families as dream killers because they fail to discover themselves and therefore cannot see the benefit they will receive from others. They are doing everything to stop others not because of what they will gain rather the aim is to stop the good work of others from coming to pass.

Exodus 20 vv16: *Thou shalt not bear false witness against thy neighbor.*

They can go to the length of lying falsely against others to make sure that they stop anything good that will come to other people, thinking that they are doing badly to others without knowing that they are doing themselves more harm.

Romans 12 v 15-25: *Rejoice with them that do rejoice, and weep with them that weep. Be of the same mind one toward another. Mind not high things, but condescend to men of low estate. Be not wise in your own conceits. Recompense to no man evil for evil. Provide things honest in the sight of all men. If it be possible, as much as lieth in you, live peaceably with all men. Dearly beloved, avenge not yourselves, but rather give place unto wrath: for it is written, Vengeance is mine; I will repay, saith the Lord. Therefore if thine enemy hunger, feed him; if he thirst, give him drink: for in so doing thou shalt heap coals of fire on his head. Be not overcome of evil, but overcome evil with good.*

But whenever you have failed to discover yourself, you might think that the breakthrough of others is your disadvantage and if you don't change this mindset and knowledge you might even fight people that God has ordained to deliver you, like Joseph's brothers who fought the man that God has destined to help their lives.

Because Joseph's brothers failed to discover themselves, they failed to understand that if Joseph becomes the king, automatically they will become king's brothers, thereby rule with him as his cabinet members which will be far much better compared to their formal position in life.

They are only fighting to stop another person without knowing that they are stopping themselves! What foolish thinking.

Luke 6 v 41-42: *And why beholdest thou the mote that is in thy brother's eye, but perceivest not the beam that is in thine own eye? Either how canst thou say to thy brother, Brother, let me pull out the mote that is in thine eye, when thou thyself beholdest not the beam that is in thine own eye? Thou hypocrite, cast out first the beam out of thine own eye, and then shalt thou see* *clearly to pull out the mote that is in thy brother's eye.*

These men failed to understand that fighting Joseph meant fighting and destroying their opportunity of becoming noble men in society. Most people you fight or criticize today is because you fail to discover your position in their life and situation.

God designed to uplift Joseph's brothers to a noble position in life but designed it that it must come through their brother Joseph. But because they failed to discover themselves, they are fighting their brother who happens to be the instrument of their greatness in life.

And as they were fighting to stop Joseph, without knowing they are fighting themselves thereby prolonging their suffering in the land of Cana.

Most people that you are fighting to stop today are the ones that God has ordained to help you out of poverty. Many people have killed their destiny helpers out of ignorance because they fail to discover themselves thereby cannot discover that the person they are suffering to frustrate is their destiny helper.

Many people that are out there crying that they have nobody to help them are suffering today because they have destroyed the destiny of people who God has positioned to help them in life simply because they failed to discover their value and that of others.

Many people that have taken an oath that nobody will be greater than them in their father's house, community, or church and will do anything possible to frustrate or stop anybody that will try to rise up from there without considering that the same person they are fighting to stop might be the person that God has ordained to save them and their generation if he/she arise to the position of power politically or financially.

Remember that God might destiny you to become the best adviser to the President while he has made the little boy from your neighborhood the President who will later appoint you into the place where you will fulfill your destiny as an adviser.

And let's assume that you have vowed that nobody around you will be better than you and you are still a common taxi driver while God has made you adviser to the President that means you can never fulfill your destiny because you have stopped the President and yourself by your wrong idea and your selfishness.

You are gossiping to make sure that your brother's daughter did not marry a wealthy person when God has ordained her to marry a governor and has ordained your son to replace the governor or to receive a good appointment from the governor, then how can it happen if the said marriage did not hold.

Esther 4 v 13-14: *Then Mordecai commanded to answer Esther, Think not with thyself that thou shalt escape in the king's house, more than all the Jews. For if thou altogether holdest thy peace at this time, then shall there enlargement and deliverance arise to the Jews from another place; but thou and thy father's house shall be destroyed: and who knoweth whether thou art come to the kingdom for such a time as this?*

Many people you are fighting today is people that God has made to be of important help to your life but because you have failed to discover yourself, you are finding it very difficult to know their value or how useful they can be to your life and ministry.

Romans 12 v 18: *If it be possible, as much as lieth in you, live peaceably with all men.*

Why? Because every human being on earth you see is very important to us one way or the other no matter how you see it. Even if you can say that the person is wicked or evil to you, if you discover yourself you will see the value of the person and use it as an advantage to your life.

Mark 16 v 15: *And he said unto them, Go ye into all the world, and preach the gospel to every creature. (Preach the gospel to the poor)*

Those that you labeled as evil, needs your help. Jesus knows that when you take the gospel to them and help them discover themselves through the word of God, they will change and become useful to themselves and to you, because the word of God is the only tool that can change and transform them into what God has made them to be and they will be useful to themselves, to society and to you.

They are fighting you simply because they don't know their value and your value. Take the word of God to them and show them how important and useful they are to God and to themselves, and you will see them change to something that will be useful and you will live to enjoy them.

Remember that they are waiting for your light to change. Enough of your silence be bold and tell them the truth, that will help them discover their real value and you will see them surrender to you and follow you to serve your God.

Bible: *If you bring your offering to the altar and find out that you are having issues without somebody leave it to go and meet them person*

You cannot please God without doing this commandment; there is no short cut in Holiness. Jesus did not say people that have something against you, least you said I have nothing against anybody rather he said if you remember that this person has something against you, meaning he knows that the person can still be of use to you and to the kingdom of God if you can win him back.

Jesus also demonstrated this at the cross when he prayed to the Father to have mercy on the people for killing him. He did this because he knew that these people doing this were helping him into his glory but they are thinking that they want to stop him.

CHAPTER SIX

Luke 4 v 18-29: *The Spirit of the Lord is upon me, because he hath anointed me to preach the gospel to the poor; he hath sent me to heal the brokenhearted, to preach deliverance to the captives, and recovering of sight to the blind, to set at liberty them that are bruised, to preach the acceptable year of the Lord. And he closed the book, and he gave it again to the minister, and sat down. And the eyes of all them that were in the synagogue were fastened on him. And he began to say unto them, this day is this scripture fulfilled in your ears. And all bare him witness, and wondered at the gracious words which* *proceeded out of his mouth. And they said, is not this Joseph's son? And he said unto them, ye will surely say unto me this proverb, Physician, heal thyself: whatsoever we have heard done in Capernaum, do also here in thy country. And he said, Verily I say unto you, no prophet is accepted in his own country. But I tell you of a truth, many widows were in Israel in the days of Elias, when the heaven was shut up three years and six months, when great famine was throughout all the land; But unto none of them was Elias sent, save unto Sarepta, a city of Sidon, unto a woman that was a widow. And many lepers were in Israel in the time of Eliseus the prophet; and none of them was cleansed, saving Naaman the Syrian. And all they in the synagogue, when they heard these things, were filled with wrath, And rose up, and thrust him out of the city, and led him unto the brow of the hill whereon their city was built, that they might cast him down headlong. But he passing through the midst of them went his way,*

Whenever you discover God's deposit in your life, know that it will not go well with people around you. They will hate you and might rise up to attack you. Do not expect people round you to applaud you whenever you discover yourself. Your deposit may attract the attack of the enemy.

And if your deposit has not attracted opposition or attacks from people around you, check very well if you are sure that you have really discovered your deposit.

From the above scripture, we understood that our Lord Jesus was attacked by his people when he discovered himself and his deposit from the word of God. The people who had been living comfortably with him from his birth turned out to attack him and try to stop him as soon as they find out that he has discovered his deposit.

They were attacking him or trying to stop him not because they wanted to step into his deposit but because they felt that they were on the same level with him or that they were better than him and for him to discover his deposit meant he will now be far ahead of them.

But they failed to understand that his discovering would be a breakthrough for all. They failed to reason from this angle because they are full of envy and jealousy not knowing that envies and jealousy will rob them the opportunity of becoming a partaker of this great breakthrough that will happen around them.

Romans 12 v 15: *Rejoice with them that do rejoice, and weep with them that weep.*

Whenever you are happy about the blessing of others, you will see the door of opportunity will be opened to you in the same blessing, and you will see where to benefit from the same miracle.

Until you deposit attracts attack, you can never be glorified. So whenever you discover yourself, expect attacks from your friends, family members, partners, and mates.

Matthew 10 v 34-36: *Think not that I am come to send peace on earth: I came not to send peace, but a sword. For I am come to set a man at variance against his father, and the daughter against her mother, and the daughter in law against her mother in law And a man's foes shall be they of his own household.*

Remember that Jesus is the word of God made flesh and it is through the word of God that you will discover yourself and whenever you discover yourself expect others who have not discovered themselves to take it as a duty to fight you.

They will fight you and make sure that they will stop you. Understand that they are fighting you because they don't know your worth and what they stand to gain from your deposit.

What they are fighting is truth which is the word of God in you.

Luke 23 v 33-34: *And when they were come to the place, which is called Calvary, there they crucified him, and the malefactors, one on the right hand, and the other on the left. Then said Jesus, Father, forgive them; for they know not what they do. And they parted his raiment, and cast lots.*

So when they are fighting you, you don't need to fight back rather understand that it is time to pray for them that God will open their eyes to see your value and their gain from your breakthrough which the devil has been hiding from them.

Matthew 5 v 44: *But I say unto you, Love your enemies, bless them that curse you, do good* *to them that hate you, and pray for them which despitefully use you, and persecute you;*

It takes your discovering from the word of God to understand that people that are fighting you are doing it to promote you and as such they deserve your prayers. The Bible says when you pray for them that God will bless you.

Know that when men are fighting you without course that they are not doing it out of hatred alone. They might love you but they are fighting to stop you from ruling over them without knowing that your ruler ship might be the only solution they desired in their life.

So you have to adhere to the teaching of Jesus and pray for them to understand the real you, which is who God has made you and not what they see or believe you are.

Because when they understand that your breakthrough is for their glory too, they will not fight you rather they will help you to achieve your glory.

Understand also that they are fighting you because they have neglected you and they have written you off in life to a level where they believed that without them you can never succeed in life.

They might be full of themselves to a level where they place themselves in the position of God and thereby have judged you and believe that nothing good can come out of you.

Isaiah 2 v 22: *Cease ye from man, whose breath is in his nostrils: for wherein is he to be accounted of?*

Philippines 4 v 13: *I can do all things through Christ which strengtheneth me.*

Most men that you are depending on for help today will rely on you tomorrow if you leave them and depend only on God for help.

The second reason why people around will fight you whenever you discover your deposit is because they will consider themselves to be more righteous and more important than you, believing that God was supposed to punish you and not to bless you.

They will consider themselves closer to know the mind of God than you. They believe that your idea is too foolish and can never take you anywhere, so they can't believe you.

Even when you tell them that such idea came from God, they can never believe you because deep in their heart they believe that there is no way God would talk to you, because to them you are unqualified, not educated, and a sinner to hear from God.

With this analysis, they believe that nothing on earth will make God reveal anything good to you. So they cannot believe your dream.

Another reason why they will fight you is because they feel that you have failed to place them in the place of authority in your vision. They want to be lord over you in your dream and whenever it does not happen the way they think, they will fight you to make sure that they stop you.

Also they might feel that they are comfortable the way they are and not ready to change to your vision.

Whenever men feel that they're comfortable with the way things are in their life, they will always find it very difficult to adapt to a new system. Whenever men feel that they are comfortable living in their sin, they will find it difficult to identify with you because of your light.

John 1 v 5: *And the light shineth in darkness; and the darkness comprehended it not.*

Remember that God's deposit upon your life is the light that lightens you when you came into this world, so whenever you discover it, the Bible says that it will shine in darkness and that darkness will not comprehend it because the light will be too difficult for them that are still in darkness to comprehend. So they will fight because they did not understand you.

1 Corinthians 2 v 9-14: *But as it is written, Eye hath not seen, nor ear heard, neither have entered into the heart of man, the things which God hath prepared for them that love him. But God hath revealed them unto us by his Spirit: for the Spirit searcheth all things, yea, and the deep things of God. For what man knoweth the things of a man, save the spirit of man which is in him? Even so the things of God knoweth no man, but the Spirit of God. Now we have received, not the spirit of the world, but the spirit which is of God;*

that we might know the things that are freely given to us of God. Which things also we speak, not in the words which man's wisdom teacheth, but which the Holy Ghost teacheth; comparing spiritual things with spiritual. But the natural man receiveth not the things of the Spirit of God: for they are foolishness unto him: neither can he know them, because they are spiritually discerned.

It will be too big for them to believe that such things can come out of you. In fact, they will doubt their ears because it will be too big to believe or understand at first.

Remember what men understands, they kill and what they don't understand, they call names! When they don't understand your light in their darkness, they will tag it with many names and try to kill it and stop you.

John 3 v 19-20: *And this is the condemnation, that light is come into the world, and men loved darkness rather than light, because their deeds were evil. For every one that doeth evil hateth the light, neither cometh to the light, lest his deeds should be reproved. But he that doeth truth cometh to the light, that his* *deeds may be made manifest, that they are wrought in God.*

The Bible says that they are doing it because their deeds are evil, so the devil must always use them to fight the light of God in you whenever you discover this light in your life.

So don't expect people around you to sing for your praises because you just discovered your deposit from the word of God. Rather have it in mind that the devil will always use people around you to fight in order to stop you.

Psalm 55 v 12-14: *For it was not an enemy that reproached me; then I could have borne it: neither was it he that hated me that did magnify himself against me; then I would have hid myself from him: But it was thou, a man mine equal, my guide, and mine acquaintance. We took sweet counsel together, and walked unto the house of God in company.*

People that you would never believe would hurt you in life will be the ones to rise up against you. They will be the first people to discourage you but always understand that your deposit makes you a carrier of God's light which will always overcomes every darkness;

Romans 16 v 33: *These things I have spoken unto you, that in me ye might have peace. In the world ye shall have tribulation: but be of good cheer; I have overcome the world.*

When Jesus said that he has overcome the world, know that the same light he used to beautify the world in creation and conquer every darkness that covers the earth is the same light he has deposited in you and with it you will overcome every challenge that will rise up whenever you discover yourself.

The light will teach you how to run your family, your job, your business, your finances, academics and everything you need in life to overcome every challenge and manifest the glory of God.

CHAPTER SEVEN

Philippians 2 v 12: *Wherefore, my beloved, as ye have always obeyed, not as in my presence only, but now much more in my absence, work out your own salvation with fear and trembling.*

Whenever you discover yourself from the word of God, you have to understand that it does not end there rather you are expected to work it out and make sure that you fulfill it.

Whenever you come to Christ in new birth, Christ will take over your soul from the devil but for the Holy Spirit to dwell in your spirit and flesh, you will be the one to work it out.

Thus, for God to fully dwell in your body and spirit must be by sanctification through his word.

John 17 v 14-24: *I have given them thy word; and the world hath hated them, because they are not of the world, even as I am not of the world. I pray not that thou shouldest take them out of the world, but that thou shouldest keep them from the evil. They are not of the world, even as I am not of the world. Sanctify them through thy truth: thy word is truth. As thou hast sent me into the world, even so have I also sent them into the world, and for their sakes I sanctify myself, that they also might be sanctified through the truth. Neither pray I for these alone, but for them also which shall believe on me through their word; That they all may be one; as thou, Father, art in me, and I in thee, that they also may be one in us: that the world may believe that thou hast sent me. And the glory which thou gavest me I have given them; that they may be one, even as we are one: I in them, and thou in me, that they may be made perfect in one; and that the world may know that thou hast sent me, and hast loved them, as thou hast loved me Father, I will that they also, whom thou hast* *given me, be with me where I am; that they may behold my glory, which thou hast given me: for thou lovedst me before the foundation of the world.*

Many have asked this question over the years. How can someone be sanctified on earth? Some people put it that we are in the world and cannot live a sin free life which is lies from the pit of hell. The Bible says that you will be sanctified through the word of God.

Your sanctification starts from when you are ready to hold and retain the word of God in your heart. Whenever you are ready to retain the word of God in your heart, whenever you are ready to do whatsoever God said to you through his word that is when your sanctification starts.

Whenever you discover through the word of God that said you should not lie and you believed it in your heart, asking God to help you overcome the spirit behind lies and to help you not to lie, the power of God in that word you believed will sanctify you. And if you have not been sanctified through the word of God, you can never work in his righteousness, because righteousness is God's own way of direction.

Righteousness is God's direction and does not depend on you to decide the state of your righteousness. Righteousness simple means working in God's revelation and direction for your life. Believing the instructions of God and trying to do them as best as you can.

Romans 4 v 3: *For what saith the scripture? Abraham believed God, and it was counted unto him for righteousness.*

Believing the revelation of God upon your life sanctifies and makes you a righteous person. When you are willing to retain any word that comes to you in your heart, the power of God in that word that you keep meditating in your heart will cleanse you from all filthiness and make you the righteousness of God

Psalm 1 v 1-3: *Blessed is the man that walketh not in the counsel of the ungodly, nor standeth in the way of sinners, nor sitteth in the seat of the scornful. But his delight is in the law of the LORD; and in his law doth he meditate day*

and night. And he shall be like a tree planted by the rivers of water, that bringeth forth his fruit in his season; his leaf also shall not wither; and whatsoever he doeth shall prosper.

Joshua 1 v 8: *This book of the law shall not depart out of thy mouth; but thou shalt meditate therein day and night, that thou mayest observe to do according to all that is written therein: for then thou shalt make thy way prosperous, and then thou shalt have good success.*

The revelation that you hear from the word will heal and bless you. Whenever you are ready to obey God's direction that you received from his word, you will definitely prosper in all your ways.

John 15 v 1-8: *I am the true vine, and my Father is the husbandman. Every branch in me that beareth not fruit he taketh away: and every branch that beareth fruit, he purgeth it, that it may bring forth more fruit. Now ye are clean through the word which I have spoken unto you. Abide in me, and I in you. As the branch cannot bear fruit of itself, except it abide in the vine; no more can ye, except ye abide in me. I am the vine, ye are the branches: He that abideth in me, and I* *in him, the same bringeth forth much fruit: for without me ye can do nothing. If a man abide not in me, he is cast forth as a branch, and is withered; and men gather them, and cast them into the fire, and they are burned. If ye abide in me, and my words abide in you, ye shall ask what ye will, and it shall be done unto you. Herein is my Father glorified, that ye bear much fruit; so shall ye be my disciples.*

Your glorification depends on your sanctification that means for you to overcome the people opposing your deposit, it must be by the revelation you received from the word of God.

The word of God you hear and try to do is what will sanctify you. When the word enters into your life, it will clear every deposit of sin and devil of your system.

2 Timothy 2 v 15: *Study to shew thyself approved unto God, a workman that needeth not to be ashamed, rightly dividing the word of truth.*

Whenever your soul and your whole system is filled with the revelation from the word of God, you will see your character changing gradually and you will begin to reject some things you hold so dear before. Things that mattered most to you before will not matter again to you because the strength to overcome sin depends on the word of God you hear and try to do.

James 1 v 22-24: *But be ye doers of the word, and not hearers only, deceiving your own selves. For if any be a hearer of the word, and not a doer, he is like unto a man beholding his natural face in a glass: For hebeholdeth himself, and goeth his way, and straightway forgetteth what manner of man he was.*

Many Christians today are enjoying hearing the word of God but not willing to do any of it. In fact, they are now so familiar with the word God to the level where they can tell you what the word says in every chapter of the scripture but they are not ready to do any of them.

2 Corinthians 3 v 6: *Who also hath made us able ministers of the New Testament; not of the letter, but of the spirit: for the letter killeth, but the spirit giveth life.*

This type people have the word of God in their head but not in their heart. Like what the word of God said in Joshua that we should meditate the word in our heart day and night, meaning that the word should be in the heart and not on the head. Because whenever the word of God is in your heart, it will show in your whole body.

2 Timothy 3 v 5: *Having a form of godliness, but denying the power thereof: from such turn away...*

Having the word of God in your head instead of your heart will not guarantee the presence of the spirit of God, because you are not ready to do what the spirit of God says through his word.

Though you might think that you know God or his people, you can never be sanctified because you are not ready to do what the spirit of God is teaching and cannot retain Christ in your heart by so doing.

You will always be thinking of evil things, your imagination will always be full of evil thoughts even when you did not like it, because you have refused to retain the word of God in your heart.

Matthew 15 v 18-19: *But those things which proceed out of the mouth come forth from the heart; and they defile the man. For out of the heart proceed evil thoughts, murders, adulteries, fornications, thefts, false witness, and blasphemies.*

Many people that are thinking of committing suicide, fornication, murder, stealing, or lying are no longer comfortable with their situation or such thinking, how to overcome this situation remains a mystery to them but the truth remains that for you to be successful and come out of any evil character, your soul must be sanctified and your soul can only be sanctified through the word of God.

When the word of God fills your soul, the word of God can now begin to direct you and tell you what to do and what not to do as a child of God.

The spirit of God will begin to speak in your heart reminding you that God is now in you and such you should not commit sin.

The presence of the spirit of God in your life will convince you that you are now a child of God and change you completely. The word of God you keeps in your heart is what will distant you from your old friends who are your partners in crime.

Whenever you have the word in you, the word will separate you from your old ways of thinking and make you to see yourself from the eyes of God, because you have discover yourself.

2 Corinthians 3 v 16-18: *Nevertheless when it shall turn to the Lord, the veil shall be taken away. Now the Lord is that Spirit: and where the Spirit of the Lord is, there is liberty. But we all, with open face beholding as in a glass the glory of the Lord, are changed into the same image from glory to glory, even as by the Spirit of the Lord.*

You will see yourself totally different from the way you used to see yourself or think of yourself before. From a condemned sinner, you will understand that you have been made the righteousness of God.

James 5 v 16-17: *Elias was a man subject to like passions as we are, and he prayed earnestly that it might not rain: and it rained not on the earth by the space of three years and six months. And he prayed again, and the heaven gave rain, and the earth brought forth her fruit.*

It is the word that determines the answers to your prayer whenever you pray. But whenever you have not retained the word of God in your heart, you can never believe in the efficacy of your prayer and you will be going around looking for who will pray for you.

But whenever you retain the word of God in your heart and be totally sanctified, you will begin to receive instant answer to your prayer whenever you pray.

Apostle James said when you retain the word of God in your heart and be sanctified that your prayer produces instant result.

Your sanctification through the word of God determines your commission in the kingdom of God. For God to bless you and you become a blessing to others depends on your sanctification through the word of God.

John 17 v 17-20: *Sanctify them through thy truth: thy word is truth. As thou hast sent me into the world, even so have I also sent them into the world? And for their sakes I sanctify myself, that they also might be sanctified through the truth. Neither pray I for these alone, but for them also which shall believe on me through their word.*

Jesus said whenever you are sanctified through his word that as the Father sent him to become a blessing to many that believe in him even so shall he send you and make you a blessing to millions of people around you.

Thus as many that will believe in your light will be blessed through you. Your sanctification gives you the right understanding of the word of God which makes the voice of God so clear to you, to the level where you can differentiate the voice of God from the voice of your flesh.

You will come to right understanding to know when your flesh is talking, when the voice of the devil is talking and when the voice of God is talking to you.

John 10 v 27-29: *My sheep hear my voice, and I know them, and they follow me: And I give* *unto them eternal life; and they shall never perish, neither shall any man pluck them out of my hand. My Father, which gave them me, is greater than all; and no man is able to pluck them out of my Father's hand.*

Meaning you will begin to hear from God the same way he hears from you when you pray. Your sanctification gives you the hearing ears to know what God is saying and at any given time, you will become a prophet to yourself and to others around you.

2 Timothy 2 v 19-22: *Nevertheless the foundation of God standeth sure, having this seal; The Lord knoweth them that are his. And, Let everyone that nameth the name of Christ depart from iniquity. But in a great house there are not only vessels of gold and of silver, but also of wood and of earth; and some to honor, and some to dishonor. If a man therefore purge himself from these, he shall be a vessel unto honor, sanctified, and meet for the master's use, and prepared unto every good work. Flee also youthful lusts: but follow righteousness, faith, charity, peace, with them that call on the Lord out of a pure heart.*

Your sanctification in life determines your honor in life and in the kingdom of God.

CHAPTER EIGHT

2 Timothy 2 v 19: *Nevertheless the foundation of God standeth sure, having this seal; The Lord knoweth them that are his. And, Let everyone that nameth the name of Christ depart from iniquity.*

Whenever you discover yourself from the word of God and you are ready to work it out to be glorified, know that foundation is one thing that you must consider so much.

Because every glory has its own kind of foundation Example; you cannot use the same foundation for downstairs and upstairs. In fact, no building contractor or engineer will advise you to do so because it can never work. Foundation is what determines the duration of any building and whenever a foundation is well controlled the building can balance and last long.

Making the glory of every building to be its foundation, which means any good building you see today, has a good foundation. So there is no doubt about it, big glory - big foundation.

Meaning whatsoever glory you see in life before you can attain it in life; you must be able to trace the kind of its foundation that carries such glory.

Luke 14 v 28-30: *For which of you, intending to build a tower, sitteth not down first, and counteth the cost, whether he has sufficient to finish it? Lest haply, after he hath laid the foundation, and is not able to finish it, all that behold it begin to mock him, Saying, This man began to build, and was not able to finish.*

Matthew 7 v 24-27: *Therefore whosoever heareth these sayings of mine, and doeth them, I will liken him unto a wise man, which built his house upon a rock: And the rain descended, and the floods came, and the winds blew, and beat upon that house; and it fell not: for it was* *founded upon a rock. And every one that heareth these sayings of mine, and doeth them not, shall be likened unto a foolish man, which built his house upon the sand: And the rain descended, and the floods came, and the winds blew, and beat upon that house; and it fell: and great was the fall of it.*

Because your failure to do this very well will lead you into laying the wrong foundation that will collapse and this will cause you to be disappointed in life.

Many companies, empires, kingdoms, families, nations, relationships, churches, organizations, banks, schools, and businesses that have collapsed were because of the wrong foundation.

Psalm 11 v 3: *If the foundations be destroyed, what can the righteous do?*

Whenever you lay the wrong foundation, no matter the kind of expert you bring to manage it, it will collapse. Nobody can save a wrong foundation when the problems come.

This is the problem that many nations are facing today. Any nation that you see crying because of bad leaders, if you trace to their foundation you will find out that they have the wrong foundation. If you trace to know why many companies, marriages, empires, kingdoms, businesses, relationships, and churches collapse, you will discover that they have the wrong foundation.

In fact, nothing kills dreams and stop destinies like the wrong foundation. Whenever many people discover their deposit, they look for people who have been so successful in that area and they admire them and wish to be like them without tracing to know their foundation.

Many people want to be like their mentor in glory but will fail to trace to the starting point or foundation of such glory.

Most people always want to identify with success or successful men and women but fail to understand that success is not a title but has a root. Any success you see, trace back to know the root.

1 John 4 v 1: *Beloved, believe not every spirit, but try the spirits whether they are of God:*

because many false prophets are gone out into the world.

Understand that not every success has its foundation from God. So when you check to know the root of the success of whosoever you are using as your mentor, you will get a clear picture of how to build such of his glory.

Philippians 3 v 10-14: *That I may know him, and the power of his resurrection, and the fellowship of his sufferings, being made conformable unto his death; if by any means I might attain unto the resurrection of the dead. Not as though I had already attained, either were already perfect: but I follow after, if that I may apprehend that for which also I am apprehended of Christ Jesus. Brethren, I count not myself to have apprehended: but this one thing I do, forgetting those things which are behind, and reaching forth unto those things which are before, I press toward the mark for the prize of the high calling of God in Christ Jesus.*

Apostle Paul having chosen Christ as his mentor, wanted to be like Christ in glory. He desired that kind of glory that made Christ to have power over all things and he understood that before that glory would come that there is a foundation required. This discovering made him to desire the suffering of Christ as well because he understood that it would be impossible to attain to such glory without passing through the same thing that Jesus passed through.

That is to say that if you do what successful people do, you will get the same result that successful people get and if you do what unsuccessful people do, you will get the same result that unsuccessful people get.

Your foundation is the right sacrifices to pay for any glory that you want to attain in life. These sacrifices might come your way in the form of shame, delay, accusation, lack, hunger, or limitation on your way of success.

Romans 8 v 35-39: *Who shall separate us from the love of Christ? Shall tribulation, or distress, or persecution, or famine, or nakedness, or peril, or sword? As it is written, for thy sake we are killed all the day long; we are accounted as sheep for the slaughter. Nay, in all these things we are more than conquerors through him that loved us. For I am persuaded, that neither death,* *nor life, nor angels, nor principalities, nor powers, nor things present, nor things to come, nor height, nor depth, nor any other creature, shall be able to separate us from the love of God, which is in Christ Jesus our Lord.*

These are the prices to pay for your glory to appear. So whenever you discover your deposit and want to attain to it in life, know that there are challenges to face on your way to attain to that greatness.

Matthew 5 v 11-12: *Blessed are ye, when men shall revile you, and persecute you, and shall say all manner of evil against you falsely, for my sake. Rejoice, and be exceeding glad: for great is your reward in heaven: for so persecuted they the prophets which were before you.*

But know that those challenges are not made to destroy you but rather to build you up for your glory to appear. So when they come your way, know that they are stepping stones for your glory.

1 Corinthians 10 v 13: *There hath no temptation taken you but such as is common to man: but God is faithful, who will not suffer you* *to be tempted above that ye are able; but will with the temptation also make a way to escape, that ye may be able to bear it.*

Men of great glory who has made it in life may have passed the same thing that you are complaining about today and they refused to give up because they understood that it was meant to build them and they endured it to the end till their glory appeared.

Matthew 10 v 22: *And ye shall be hated of all men for my name's sake: but he that endureth to the end shall be saved.*

That means for you to be like Christ and overcome all your troubles in life, know that you must be ready to accept and identify with what he has passed through and be ready to endure them like him.

1 Timothy 3 v 16: *And without controversy great is the mystery of godliness: God was manifest in the flesh, justified in the Spirit, seen of angels, preached unto the Gentiles, believed on in the world, received up into glory.*

Know that whatsoever thing that you see under the heaven was created by the Holy Spirit of God and you have that same Holy Spirit in you now. So for you to build your life, marriage, business, finances, career, relationship, etc. it must be by the same spirit of God in you.

All you need to do is to sit down and think of the kind of life, marriage, business, finances, career, relationship and glory you want to build, then trace the foundation attached to it and ask the Holy Spirit to help you overcome the temptation attached to such glory and he will do it for you; that is why God sent him for you.

1 John 2 v 27: *But the anointing which ye have received of him abideth in you, and ye need not that any man teach you: but as the same anointing teacheth you of all things, and is truth, and is no lie, and even as it hath taught you, ye shall abide in him.*

Because God has given you the anointing that will teach you how to build any glory with an excellent foundation and guide you to make quality and intelligent decisions without further mistakes.

Isaiah 30 v 21: *And thine ears shall hear a word behind thee, saying, this is the way, walk ye* *in it, when ye turn to the right hand, and when ye turn to the left.*

If only you will listen to the Holy Spirit at all times, you can never make any wrong choices because he will always teach you what to do at all time.

The anointing is assigned to lead you to overcome all your fear, failures, limitations, and every problem in your foundation. God will explain your deposit and foundation attached to it to your understanding, because he wants to work with you and help you to achieve them. All you need to do is to listen and allow him lead you.

Romans 12 v 11: *Not slothful in business; fervent in spirit; serving the Lord.*

And you have to be up and doing whenever you want to work with him. Know that the time of your foundation is time of your prayer and a Holy living.

And you can now be sure to overcome the level where the devil will no longer trouble your heart with your problems.

You grow to a level where you will no longer allow him to trouble you again with those things that he has been using to cause your heart not to be at peace.

Thus, those things that he has been using to torment your heart for many years in the past no longer bothers you, because your believe in God has conquered all your fear over the devil and his attacks.

Meaning his power over you have been broken and you are sure that you have laid a solid foundation of any kind of glory you wants in life and knowing full well that it must survive.

Joshua 1 v 8: *This book of the law shall not depart out of thy mouth; but thou shalt meditate therein day and night, that thou mayest observe to do according to all that is written therein: for then thou shalt make thy way prosperous, and then thou shalt have good success.*

Whenever you want to create your kingdom, empire, family, business, etc. with the word of God, know that it will stand the test of time because you have built it upon Christ which is the eternal rock of ages which no wind can destroy.

2 Timothy 2 v 19: *Nevertheless the foundation of God standeth sure, having this seal; The Lord knoweth them that are his. And, let everyone that nameth the name of Christ depart from iniquity.*

Your foundation will stand because you have the seal of God upon it and no demon can bring it down.

Job 22 v 29: *When men are cast down, then thou shalt say, there is lifting up; and he shall save the humble person*

And you will have all around peace that will make you to feel peace. When others are complaining of economic meltdown, you will be sleeping because you have your foundation on God. That is why you have to lay your foundation on God.

Chapter Nine

Psalm 149 v 5-9: *Let the saints be joyful in glory: let them sing aloud upon their beds. Let the high praises of God be in their mouth, and a two-edged sword in their hand; to execute vengeance upon the heathen, and punishments upon the people; to bind their kings with chains, and their nobles with fetters of iron; to execute upon them the judgment written: this honor have all his saints. Praise ye the* LORD.

The devil does not fear you rather it fears the word of God that you know. That is what he is afraid of and whenever you do not know or retain the word of God in your heart, the devil will always fight you because he knows that you can never fight back.

Devil will always conquer people who are not ready to conquer him.

1 Peter 5 v 8: *Be sober, be vigilant; because your adversary the devil, as a roaring lion, walketh about, and seeking whom he may devour.*

The Bible says that he is moving around looking for whom to destroy. That is true but he will only destroy people that have refused to retain the word of God in their heart. Because it is the word of God that you know that gives you power over the devil.

Hebrews 4 v 12-13: *For the word of God is quick, and powerful, and sharper than any two edged sword, piercing even to the dividing asunder of soul and spirit, and of the joints and marrow, and is a discerner of the thoughts and intents of the heart. Neither is there any creature that is not manifest in his sight: but all things are naked and opened unto the eyes of him with whom we have to do.*

The word of God you know makes you to understand the destiny of the devil and where he belongs, which will give you power to live above him. And whenever he tries to make you afraid in any way, you will let him know that he has been judged and you have been given power to execute his sentience that is already passed on him because this is part of your destiny in Christ.

When you retain the word of God in your heart, the devil can never attack you because he knows your destiny which is to execute his sentience and his destiny that he has been judged, so he will always be afraid of you.

Because whenever he tries to raise his head on you, you will destroy him by the word of God that you know.

When you speak the word of God that is in your heart, you can kill any demon around. The word of God you know is a sword of the spirit and is made to kill the devils and very evil spirit on the air, sea and everywhere.

The devil knows that the word can kill him and that is why he can't play with anyone that has it in his heart.

Revelations 12 v 11: *And they overcame him by the blood of the Lamb and by the word of their testimony; and they loved not their lives unto the death.*

Your power over the devil, sin and every weakness in life, marriage, business, finance, academics, relationships, and character comes from the word of God you know. Whenever you are filled with his word, you will be rest assured of yourself that you can stand firm against the devil and all his traps.

Matthew 4 v 1-11: *Then was Jesus led up of the Spirit into the wilderness to be tempted of the devil. And when he had fasted forty days and forty nights, he was afterward an hungred. And when the tempter came to him, he said, if thou be the Son of God, command that these stones be made bread. But he answered and said, it is written, Man shall not live by bread alone, but by every word that proceeded out of the mouth of God. Then the devil taketh him up into the holy city, and setteth him on a pinnacle of the temple,*

And saith unto him, If thou be the Son of God, cast thyself down: for it is written, He shall give his angels charge concerning thee: and in their hands they shall bear thee up, lest at any time thou dash thy foot against a stone. Jesus said unto him, it is written again, Thou shalt not tempt the Lord thy God. Again, the devil taketh him up into an exceeding high mountain, and showeth him all the kingdoms of the world, and the glory of them; And saith unto him, All these things will I give thee, if thou wilt fall down and worship me. Then saith Jesus unto him, Get thee hence, Satan: for it is written, Thou shalt worship the Lord thy God, and him only shalt thou serve. Then the devil leaveth him, and, behold, angels came and ministered unto him.

Jesus was able to defeat the devil because of the word of God that he knew and spoke.

Luke 2 v 52: *And Jesus increased in wisdom and stature and in favour with God and man.*

Meaning whenever you have the word of God in you, there will be all around growth in every area of your life and in all you do. Thus, for you to grow in your spirit, business, finances and status, it must be through the word of God.

Matthew 6 v 27: *Which of you by taking thought can add one cubit unto his stature?*

For growth to take place in any area of your life, it must happen by the approval of the word of God that is why Jesus said in John 1 v 1 that nothing made was made without (the word) him.

And this is where many people got it wrong by thinking that they can achieve anything without the word of God. Whenever you understand that the power to achieve everything you need or whatsoever thing that you are looking for in life is in the word of God, then you will live to make the word of God a standard for your life. Because whatsoever thing you wants here on earth is found in the word of God or whatsoever you want to create or build can be done through the word of God. Be it peace, money, kingdom, empire, etc.

Whenever you understand that the power to live above every enemy has been given to you in the word of God. Then you will clinch to the word of God.

Ephesians 5 v 18-20: *And be not drunk with wine, wherein is excess; but be filled with the Spirit; Speaking to yourselves in psalms and hymns and spiritual songs, singing and making melody in your heart to the Lord; Giving thanks always for all things unto God and the Father in the name of our Lord Jesus Christ.*

So for you to receive anything through the word of God, you must be ready to activate the power of the word of God.   And for you to experience the release of the power of God in your life, you must declare God's word which will cause your faith to grow and give you power to overcome the devil and pleasure of the word.

Jesus was able to stand bold against the devil after showing him the glory of the whole world and overcome him by the word because faith to overcome the world comes from the word of God you know, the word of God you know is the spirit of God in you.

Faith is the decision to keep the word of God in you and it is based on the meditation of the word.

Matthew 12 v 33-35: *Either make the tree good, and his fruit good; or else make the tree corrupt, and his fruit corrupt: for the tree is known by his fruit. O generation of vipers, how can ye, being evil, speak good things? For out of the abundance of the heart the mouth speaketh. A good man out of the good treasure of the heart bringeth forth good things: and an evil man out of the evil treasure bringeth forth evil things.*

Whenever you keep the word in your heart, it will reflect in your mouth, because you will always speak what you believe in your heart. Jesus said out of the abundance of the heart because he knew that whenever you have the word of God deeply in your heart, you will always speak the word of God to your situation.

Then the word of God which is the spirit of God will always work through you making the devil to be far from anything that concerns you because whenever you speak it, you activate the power that can kill him.

2 Timothy 2 v 15: *Study to shew thyself approved unto God, a workman that needeth not to be ashamed, rightly dividing the word of truth.*

You will not be ashamed to speak over any situation because you know what to do and you will receive the necessary result.

Romans 1 v 16: *For I am not ashamed of the gospel of Christ: for it is the power of God unto salvation to everyone that believeth; to the Jew first, and also to the Greek.*

Many Christians that fail to retain the word of God in their heart are ashamed to pray for a sick person in public or even afraid to pray for themselves in secret because they are empty and don't have the word of God in them and for that reason, the devil will make them believe that they are powerless to pray or that the Holy spirit cannot help them.

They fail to remember that they weren't made right with God because of their own righteousness, that righteousness came because God gave them His righteousness.

Thus, His presence with man isn't dependent on what you did right or wrong, or the way you feel; His presence is dependent on His infallible word that you retain in your heart.

Hebrews 13v 5-6: *Let your conversation be without covetousness; and be content with such things as ye have: for he hath said, I will never leave thee, nor forsake thee. So that we may boldly say, The Lord is my helper, and I will not fear what man shall do unto me.*

That's the reason He'll never leave you nor forsake you. As long as you haven't willfully rejected Christ and His sacrifice of salvation for you on the cross, the Holy Spirit cannot and will not leave you when you retain his word any time in your heart.

That is why Apostle Paul said, "I am not afraid of the devil because whenever I declare the word, the same word is the power of God that will cause that deliverance to take place, thus when I speak the word I activate the power of God because I keep the word in my heart."

James 5 v 16: *Confess your faults one to another, and pray one for another, that ye may be healed. The effectual fervent prayer of a righteous man availeth much. Elias was a man subject to like passions as we are, and he prayed earnestly that it might not rain: and it rained not on the earth by the space of three years and six* *months. And he prayed again, and the heaven gave rain, and the earth brought forth her fruit.*

The devil knows that whenever you speak the word, that you activate the power of God. Instead, he will always want you to be afraid and never to believe in your prayers. The devil does not want you to believe your prayer or the word of God in your mouth.

But Apostle James said that you should never mind him because your prayer is working. So never think that your prayers are not working as long as you have the word of God in your mouth to back it up.

It is wrong for you to think that your prayers are not working. He knows that your right understanding of this will destroy him; he is afraid of the word of God because the word is the sword of the spirit and it will always destroy him.

Colossians 2 v 14-15: *Blotting out the handwriting of ordinances that was against us, which was contrary to us, and took it out of the way, nailing it to his cross; and having spoiled* *principalities and powers, he made a shew of them openly, triumphing over them in it.*

You need the right knowledge of the word of God in you to destroy the devil and expose all of his works in your life. Through the word, every enemy of your life will be exposed and their works destroy.

1 John 2 v 27: *But the anointing which ye have received of him abideth in you, and ye need not that any man teaches you: but as the same anointing teacheth you of all things, and is truth, and is no lie, and even as it hath taught you, ye shall abide in him.*

Anointing from the word of God will teach you how to stand and outshine them at all times. Meaning in the face of any problem, the anointing will teach you how to overcome them.

You will not need to struggle to run your family, business, marriage, or finances because the anointing that will come from the right knowledge of the word of God will teach you how to overcome always.

The devil fears them that fear God and respect them that respect God and obey them that obey and keep the word of God in their heart.

That means whenever you are ready to obey God by keeping his word in your heart, it will be impossible for the devil to attack you and anything that belongs to you. Attacking you will be attacking God which the devil knows that he cannot win, so he will not even try it.

John 10 v 11-18: *I am the good shepherd: the good shepherd giveth his life for the sheep. But he that is an hireling, and not the shepherd, whose own the sheep are not, seeth the wolf coming, and leaveth the sheep, and fleeth: and the wolf catcheth them, and scattereth the sheep. The hireling fleeth, because he is an hireling, and careth not for the sheep. I am the good shepherd, and know my sheep, and am known of mine. As the Father knoweth me, even so know I the Father: and I lay down my life for the sheep. And other sheep I have, which are not of this fold: them also I must bring, and they shall hear my voice; and there shall be one fold, and one shepherd. Therefore doth my Father love me, because I lay down my life, that I might take it again? No man taketh it from me, but I lay it* *down of myself. I have power to lay it down, and I have power to take it again. This commandment have I received of my Father.*

Meaning whenever you have the word of God, the devil will always see you as God and he will respect you as he respects God.

Whenever he sees you, he will tread very careful and whenever he sees anything that concerns you, he will keep off because he knows that touching you means touching the apple of God's eyes and that God will not take it lightly.

Whenever he tries it, God will arise to defend you. So the devil won't give his agents charge to touch you and your property.

Nahum 1 v 9: *What do ye imagine against the LORD? He will make an utter end: affliction shall not rise up the second time.*

The mark of God upon your life will always speak for you before cultic men and women and they can never engage you in trouble because they know that you process the presence of God.

Mark 5 v 1-20: *And they came over unto the other side of the sea, into the country of the*

Gadarenes. And when he was come out of the ship, immediately there met him out of the tombs a man with an unclean spirit, Who had his dwelling among the tombs; and no man could bind him, no, not with chains: Because that he had been often bound with fetters and chains, and the chains had been plucked asunder by him, and the fetters broken in pieces: neither could any man tame him. And always, night and day, he was in the mountains, and in the tombs, crying, and cutting himself with stones. But when he saw Jesus afar off, he ran and worshipped him, And cried with a loud voice, and said, what have I to do with thee, Jesus, thou Son of the most high God? I adjure thee by God, that thou torment me not. For he said unto him, Come out of the man, thou unclean spirit. And he asked him, what is thy name? And he answered, saying, my name is Legion: for we are many. And he besought him much that he would not send them away out of the country. Now there was there nigh unto the mountains a great herd of swine feeding. And all the devils besought him, saying; Send us into the swine, that we may enter into them. And forthwith Jesus gave them leave. And the unclean spirits went out, and entered into the swine: and the herd ran violently down a steep place into the sea, (they were about two thousand ;) and were choked in the sea. And they that fed the swine fled, and told it in the city, and in the country. And they went out to see what it was that was done. And they come to Jesus, and see him that was possessed with the devil, and had the legion, sitting, and clothed, and in his right mind: and they were afraid. And they that saw it told them how it befell to him that was possessed with the devil, and also concerning the swine. And they began to pray him to depart out of their coasts. And when he was come into the ship, he that had been possessed with the devil prayed him that he might be with him. Howbeit Jesus suffered him not, but saith unto him, Go home to thy friends, and tell them how great things the Lord hath done for thee, and hath had compassion on thee? And he departed, and began to publish in Decapolis how great things Jesus had done for him: and all men did marvel.

Even a demon possessed person will be delivered at your wish. This man had been in this condition for so many years without choice or help. But when he saw Jesus the Bible says he ran and fell at his feet, because the demon in him had noticed the presence of God in Jesus.

The man knew that apart from a person like Jesus who is the express image of the Father, nobody can help him. The word of God that you retain in you makes you a savor to others.

The word makes people depend on you as their last hope. Whenever things are very tough they will begin to look for you to come and deliver them because you are a Lord over every bad situation.

John 14 v 12: *Verily, verily, I say unto you, He that believeth on me, the works that I do shall he do also; and greater works than these shall he do; because I go unto my Father.*

Notice that Jesus was not talking to everybody but to his disciples, people that are ready to keep his word in their heart. Because when you have the word in you, you will do great work, because his word is the only thing that every situation obeys and people that has it has his spirit which the devil must obey.

Zechariah 6 v 15: *And they that are far off shall come and build in the temple of the LORD,* *and ye shall know that the* LORD *of hosts hath sent me unto you. And this shall come to pass, if ye will diligently obey the voice of the* LORD *your God.*

Your body is the temple of God and whenever you retain the word of God in your heart, people from afar will help you build and help you fulfill your destiny.

Study to discover your deposit, retain the word of God in your heart, and it will make God take you out every captive to crown you king over your situation because retaining his word in your heart will keep you connected as a branch to the tree which Christ.

When you stay connected to him, you will bring fruit that makes you rule your world and that is his will for your life, to discover your deposit and use it to rule the earth and have dominion over all things.

Other Books
By Evangelist HARRISON
JOHNSON UCHE

Kingdom of God In You

How to Attract Your Desired Change

Gospel In Your Character

www.ingramcontent.com/pod-product-compliance
Lightning Source LLC
Chambersburg PA
CBHW061736050726
47598CB00002B/497